Wild Flowers of Cornwall

Trevor & Endymion Beer

Introduction

The Cornish cliffs, dunes and hedgerows have an abundance of wildflowers. This simple guide will help you to identify many of them and increase your enjoyment when exploring the countryside. Plants are arranged by the colour of the flower with brief plant descriptions and details of local names, habitats and ancient uses.

Please remember not to pick wildflowers – leave them for everyone to enjoy. Many provide food for insects, birds and other animals. Try to keep to footpaths wherever possible and do remember the Country Code and the tide times!

May you have many happy hours enjoying Cornwall's magnificent scenery with its abundance of wildflowers and plants.

For further information of all the titles in this series please visit:-
www.tormark.co.uk

Designed by Alix Wood,
www.alixwood.co.uk

Published by
Tor Mark, United Downs Ind Est, Redruth,
Cornwall TR16 5HY
First published 2010: reprinted 2016

ISBN 978 085025 419 8

Printed by Booths Print, The Praze, Penryn,
Cornwall TR10 8AA

Bell Heather *Erica cinerea*

Low evergreen shrub up to 60cm, similar to *Heather* (p6) in habit. Smooth leaves in whorls of three or four shoots in the leaf axils. The bell-shaped corolla tube has eight stamens hidden inside. Flowers are pollinated by bees and are usually a strongly rich purple and often found growing with *Heather*

Local Names: Honey Bottle, Bell Ling

Habitat: Well drained, poor, sandy soil. Damp habitats, heaths and moorlands; and with ling creates a purple landscape

Bramble Flower *Rubus fruticosus*

There are more than 300 species of bramble. Common and widespread. Flowers pinkish-white. Stems are thick, prickly and sprawling

Flowers: May-September

Local Names: Yoe-Brimmel, Mushes

Ancient Uses: The fruit is used to make bramble jelly, blackberry and apple pie, eaten raw with cream, used in fruit dessert jellies and in other culinary ways

Habitat: Commons, hedgerows, scrub, heaths, woodlands, cliffs, waste ground

Broad Leaved Everlasting Pea *Lathyrus latifolius*

A garden escape now naturalised. Large magenta-pink flowers, occasionally white and rather sweet-pea like. Long, fairly broad leaflets in pairs with tendrils at the top of the whole leaf. Tendrils wind around other vegetation helping the plant to climb

Flowers: June-August

Habitat: Railways, hedges, thickets, banks

Common Vetch *Vicia sativa*

Originally introduced from the continent. Short-stalked pink-purple flowers. Four-eight pairs of narrow leaflets on slender stems. Branched tendrils at the tip of the leaves helping the plant to climb 15-120cm

Flowers: May-September
Habitat: Grassy places, disturbed ground, open hedgerows

Creeping Thistle *Cirsium arvense*

A perennial spreading by means of underground stems, not just by fertilised seed distribution. (Female and male flowers usually occur on separate plants) Fluffy, rounded, pink-lilac or purple flower heads in clusters of up to five or solitary. Prickly, alternate leaves

Flowers: July-September
Habitat: Meadows and pastures, waste ground

Cuckoo Flower *Cardamine pratensis*

Pale pink, lilac or white flowers, blossoming at the time the cuckoo arrives from Africa to lay her eggs in the nests of other birds. Grows 20-60cm and is a hairless perennial. An important food plant for caterpillars of the Orange Tip butterfly and the Green Veined White butterfly

Flowers: April-June
Local Names: Ladies Smock, Milk Maids
Habitat: Damp meadows, roadsides, moist grassy places, stream banks

Dog Rose *Rosa canina*

Among a variety of wild roses are the dog roses - these have pink or white flowers.
Flowers: June-July
Local Names: Canker, Canker Rose, Humack, Pig-rose, Pig's Rose, Rose Briar, Yoe Brimble
Ancient Uses: Rose hips, found in early autumn, are still used to make rosehip jelly or syrup, rich in Vitamin C
Habitat: Hedgerows, scrub, woodland margins and thickets

Foxglove *Digitalis purpurea*

Grows 1-2m, the foxglove is an erect, leafy plant. Flowers are large drooping bells, pink to purple with dark spots
Flowers: June-September
Local Names: Cowflop, Flop-a-dock, Green Pops, Pop Dock, Pop Glove, Poppy-dock.
Ancient Uses: In 1785 William Withering discovered that digitalis found in the leaves prevented heart disease
Habitat: Hedge banks, lane verges, river banks, scrub, open heathland, rocky hillsides

Great Willowherb *Epilobium hirsutum*

Great Willowherb is very hairy, stout and grows 80-180cm. The leaves are coarsely toothed and mostly opposite.
The flowers are a bright purplish pink
Flowers: July-August
Local Names: Apple-pie, Cherry-pie, Codlins, Gooseberry-pie, Sugar Codlins, Wild Phlox (Codlins are a kind of apple)
Habitat: Cultivated wasteland, woodlands, ditches, rocky places and common by stream sides and damp places

Heather/Ling *Calluna vulgaris*

Small shrub usually under 60cm high. Branched stems rooting at the base. Pink to purple flowers, occasionally white - the 'lucky white heather'. Heather honey is a popular delicacy. Hive bees are often taken to areas of heather when it is in full flower

Flowers: July-September

Local Names: Bissom, Mountain Mist

Habitat: Heaths, moorland, bogs and roadsides, woodland banks where there is acid soil

Hemp Agrimony *Eupatorium cannabinum*

Pinkish-purple flowers develop with protruding stamens and are massed together, forming broad flat-topped clusters. Grows 90-150cm

Flowers: July-September

Local Names: Black Elder, Virgin Mary

Ancient Uses: Clears the body of catarrh and coughs, and helps with urinary problems and jaundice

Habitat: Hedgerows, damp woods, pond and river sides, marshes, ditches and scrub

Herb Robert *Geranium robertianum*

An annual with hairy stems and leaves which may be green tinged with red, sometimes completely red. The leaves are fern-like and the flowers are pink. A strong smelling plant growing from 10-50cm

Flowers: May-September

Local Names: Bird's Eye, Robin's Eye, Wren, Bachelor's Buttons, Gipsy Flower, Gipsies

Ancient Uses: To treat blood disorders. Leaves were used to staunch the flow of blood

Habitat: Hedge banks, woodlands, old walls, rocks, coasts

Ivy Leaved Toadflax *Cymbalaria muralis*

A small trailing plant growing up to 60cm in length. Long slender stems adorned with small ivy-shaped leaves, growing alternately along the stem, which are rather fleshy. Flowers are tiny snapdragon blossoms of lilac to mauvish violet with a yellow patch
Flowers: May-September
Local Names: Mother of Thousands/Millions, Nanny Goat's Mouth, Roving Sailor
Habitat: Old walls, stony hedge banks, woods, pavements, rocky places

Knapweed *Centaurea nigra*

Perennial with tough branching stems 30-60cm high. Distinguished from thistles by the absence of prickles. Bright pink-purple flowers. A favourite nectar plant of butterflies, bees and other insects
Flowers: June-September
Ancient Uses: Used for wounds, ruptures, sores, bruises and sore throats. Once used for love divination
Habitats: Hedgerows, railway embankments, roadsides, scrub, meadows, grassy places including coastal fields

Musk Thistle *Carduus nutans*

Half nodding bright purple-reddish flower heads with numerous spine tipped flower bracts. It is thought the scent of the flower is reminiscent of musk or almonds. The plant is erect, spiny with alternate leaves and is a biennial. Occurs on well drained calcareous soil. Grows up to one metre
Flowers: May-September
Local Names: Nodding Thistle
Habitat: Grassy places, roadsides, arable land, banks by rivers

Purple Loosestrife *Lythrum salicaria*

Blossoms are long spikes consisting of numerous purple flowers each with six narrow petals. The plant forms in clumps and has erect stems. Unstalked, opposite leaves which are spear-shaped to oval. Altogether a grey-green hairy plant
Flowers: June-August
Local Names: Long Purples, Emmet's (ant's) Stalk
Habitat: Damp places, ditches, marshes, dykes

Purple Toadflax *Linaria purpurea*

A perennial growing 60-90cm. Originally a garden escape but now naturalised. Hairless slender plant with deeply rich, purple-violet flowers that are small, numerous and snap-dragon shaped making up branched dense cone heads
Flowers: June-August
Habitat: Walls, Stony waste ground, banks and dry hedges

Pyramidal Orchids *Anacamptis pyramidalis*

Pale pink-purplish flowers, rarely white, form in dense pyramidal-conical shaped heads. Growing 20-45cm high. An upright hairless plant with spear-shaped leaves. Pollinated by insects, the plant provides a good source of nectar for both day and night flying insects
Flowers: June-August
Habitat: Scrub, grassy places, coastal dunes, roadsides, downland

Ragged Robin *Lychnis flos-cuculi*

Slender erect stems with long slender opposite leaves. Grows 20-70cm. Flowers are bright purplish-pink. Named Ragged Robin after the four narrow lobes which comprise each petal and give an extremely ragged look
Flowers: May-August
Local Names: Bachelor's Buttons
Ancient Uses: Used in love divination and to decorate garlands and crowns
Habitat: Wet woodland, marshes, stream-sides and damp meadows

Red Bartsia *Odontites vernus*

An erect and hairy plant, grey-green with unstalked, toothed and paired leaves. Grows 10-30cm. Pink-purple two-toned flowers which may be reddish pink or occasionally white. Flowers form on leafy spikes and usually face the same way on each spikelet
Flowers: July-October
Ancient Uses: as a cure for toothache
Habitat: Grassy & waste places, scrub, roadsides, seashores, salt marshes, meadows

Restharrow *Ononis repens*

Hairy perennial with bright pink flowers and low growing habit, with woody, often creeping root system, sometimes spiny. It was known for 'arresting the harrow', hence its English name
Flowers: June-September
Local Names: Cat-whin, Horses-breath, Lewte, Stayplough
Ancient Uses: The roots were chewed by children as 'wild liquorice'
Habitat: Grasslands and sand dune systems

Rock Sea Spurrey *Spurgularia rupicola*

A perennial with hairy stems and leaves which are also sticky. Petals are about the same length as the sepals. Pink-purple flowers. Un-winged seeds. The leaves are narrow and slightly pointed, fanned against the stems and all the way down the main stems

Flowers: June-September

Local Names: Also known as Cliff and sand spurrey

Habitat: Found around rocky coasts, in walls close to the sea, in short turf, broken ground and scree

Rosebay Willowherb *Chamerion angustifolium*

Long slender alternate leaves, very slightly toothed, pointed and hairless. Plant grows 80-150cm. Flowers are many, deep pink-purple, forming large spikes

Flowers: June-September

Ancient Uses: A sacred plant never to be picked - 'Herb of Heaven'

Habitat: Hedgerows, railway embankments, riverbanks, woodland margins, fire sites, felled woodland, and waste ground

Sea Bindweed *Calystegia soldanella*

Petals are fused together to form the large solitary trumpet-like or funnel-shaped flowers. Creeping not climbing stems. Small rounded kidney-shaped leaves. Leaves are alternate. Pink-purplish flowers usually with white stripes. Can grow up to one metre but does not fasten on to other plants. Fruits are capsules full of seeds

Flowers: June-August

Habitat: Common in stabilised sand dunes and coastal areas of sand and shingle

Sea Rocket *Cakile maritima*

Grows up to 60cm, leaves fleshy and blue-green. A hairless plant. Flowers pink, violet or whitish and scented. Prefers the drift line of a sandy beach but may be found in dunes or on shingle. The succulent leaves conserve all the fresh water they can find. Can tolerate being buried by sand. Annual
Flowers: June-September
Habitat: Seashores, shingle may be found on coastal rocks

Spear Thistle *Cirsium vulgare*

A biennial growing 80-150cm. Common and widespread. Stiff, prickly stems with uneven spiny wings. Clustered red-purple flower heads. Alternate prickly leaves, the whole plant being dull green, but is much brighter when the flowers come into bloom. Pollinated by bees, butterflies and other insects who love it for the rich source of nectar
Flowers: July-October
Habitat: Grassy places, disturbed soil, waste ground, roadsides and cultivated land

Thrift *Armeria maritima*

Tufted perennial with rosettes of grass-like leaves, hairy flowering stems without leaves and solitary pink flower-heads. All parts of individual flowers in fives
Flowers: March-October
Local Names: Brittons, Cliff Rose, Lady's Cushion, Midsummer Fairmaid, Sea Pink
Habitat: Common on cliffs and in muddy or sandy places along the coast. Often found carpeting large areas of cliffs

Tree Mallow *Lavatera arborea*

Stout biennial with stems woody at the base. May grow to 3m. Flowers are large and pink-purple with dark centres.There are numerous stamens

Flowers: June-September
Local Names: Sea Mallow, Wild Hollyhock.
Ancient Uses: Used against sprains, 'steeped in water and laid on the injury'
Habitat: Sea cliffs, stony ground, waste ground, stabilised dunes

Wild Basil *Clinopodium vulgare*

This plant has square stems, is slightly aromatic and is covered in soft hairs. Grows 40-75cm. The leaves are opposite and mostly oval. The deep pink to purple flowers form in dense whorls above each pair of upper-most leaves

Flowers: July-September
Habitat: Hedgerows, scrub, open woodland, banks, grassy meadows, dry places

Wild Thyme *Thymus praecox (also known as Thymus polytrichus and T.drucei)*

Low growing faintly sweet-smelling perennial with long creeping stems. Rich purple flowers forming in dense heads with protruding stamens

Flowers: May-September
Local Names: Mother Thyme, Tea Grass
Ancient Uses: For headaches and giddiness The scent gives strength and courage
Habitat: Heaths, short turf, dry grassy, sandy or rocky places and often found on ant-hills

Dog Rose

Common Scurvy Grass *Cochlearia officinalis*

Low growing plant with four-petalled white flowers and smooth, fleshy leaves which contain vitamin C. Leaves heart or kidney shaped, lower ones forming a rosette. Seed pods globe shaped. Flowers white or lilac

Flowers: May-August

Ancient Uses: Against scurvy, both as a medicine and in sandwiches

Habitat: Common along roadsides and often carpeting salt marshes and coastal estuarine sites

Enchanter's Nightshade *Circaea lutetiana*

Grows 30-60cm. Flowers are delicate, tiny white or pinkish and adorn slender, usually branched stems. The petals are deeply notched

Flowers: June-August

Ancient Uses: Thought to be a magical plant. Once was used against spells cast by elves

Habitat: Woodland, coppices, shaded places, cultivated land, woodland banks and hedgerows

Eyebright *Euphrasia nemorosa*

Grows 10-25cm, has branched stems and two lipped white or pale lilac flowers, with a splash of yellow and purple veins. Leaves are deeply toothed and almost triangular in shape

Flowers: June-September

Local Names: Bird's Eye

Ancient Uses: Used to heal eye complaints

Habitat: Grassland, open woodland, sand dunes, heaths

Garlic Mustard *Alliaria petiolata*

A hairy plant with stiff, slender stems and alternate leaves. The leaves are heart-shaped, short stalked, toothed and smell of garlic when crushed. Flowers are white and clustered

Flowers: April-June
Local Names: Jack-by-the-Hedge
Ancient Uses: Used to make a sauce for fish, and as a green or in salads
Habitat: Hedgerows, open woodlands, waste ground, scrub, roadsides, wood margins

Greater Stitchwort *Stellaria holostea*

Grows 30-60cm and often forms in patches. Branched spreading, straggling stems, untoothed, narrow opposite leaves

Flowers: April-June
Local Names: Satin Flower, Adder's Meat, Adder's Spit, Lady's Smock, Ladies White Petticoats, Old Man's Shirt, Pixie Flower
Ancient Uses: Used against the 'stitch', a sudden pain or pricking in the side
Habitat: Hedgerows, embankments, woodland margins, grassy places

Hedge Bindweed *Calystegia sepium*

A vigorous, hairless plant with arrow-shaped, untoothed and stalked alternate leaves. The stems are twining and climbing, and the plant grows up to 3m high. Flowers are large white trumpets with yellow centres. Pollinated by insects, particularly bumble bees. Hedge Bindweed can be a troublesome garden weed but because it has short roots is easy to pull up

Flowers: July-September
Local Names: Bellbine
Habitat: Hedgerows, scrub, marshes and woodland margins

Cow/Hedge Parsley *Anthriscus sylvestris*

Grows 80-150cm. Delicate scented flowers are lace-like and white. Flower heads are branched so that the small circular clusters of tiny flowers form a larger, loosely circular flower head
Flowers: April-June
Local Names: Queen Anne's Lace
Ancient Uses: Fodder for pigs, often mixed with bracken tops and blackberry tips
Habitat: Hedgerows woodland margins, roadside verges, grassy places

Hemlock Water Dropwort *Oenanthe crocata*

Has white, numerous flowers making up large umbels. Stems are thick, grooved and hollow. The leaves are parsley-like with broad segments. May grow to over a metre
Flowers: June-July
Local Names: Bilders
Ancient Uses: Poisonous but once used to poultice the galled (sores caused by constant rubbing) backs of horses
Habitat: Wet woodlands and ditches, rivers, streams and boggy places

Lesser Stitchwort *Stellaria graminea*

A finer plant than the *Greater Stitchwort* (p15) with smaller flowers that have more divided petals. A perennial inhabiting well drained acid type soils. Pollinated by flies and a member of the 'Pink' family
Flowers: May-August
Habitat: Grassland, woodland rides, and hedge banks

Meadow Sweet *Filipendula ulmaria*

An upright perennial growing 70-120cm with large fluffy creamy flower heads that are made up of clusters of numerous flowers. Flowers are deep sweet-musk scented. Leaves are divided or pinnate, white and hairy underneath. Large lower leaves have up to five pairs of leaflets. Leaves are toothed
Flowers: June-September
Ancient Uses: Best known for its use against malaria
Habitat: Wet meadows, marshes, roadsides, woodland margins

Ox-Eye Daisy *Leucanthemum vulgare*

Large solitary daisy flowers with erect stems. Leaves are broadly toothed and dark green. Grows 20-60cm
Flowers: June-August
Local Names: Moon Daisy, Dog Daisy, Bull's Eye, Gadjevraws (Cornish for great daisy), Horse Daisy
Ancient Uses: Against wounds and ulcers. Used in a drink to cure breathing problems such as asthma and against consumption
Habitat: Grassy banks, meadows, roadsides and rough grassland

Pignut *Conopodium majus*

Grows 20-40cm. Has very fine fern-feather like leaves. The flowers are white, delicate, lace-like and form in loose umbels
Flowers: May-July
Local Names: Earthnut, Varenut, Fern-Nut, Grovenut, Killimore, Underground Nut
Ancient Uses: The 'nuts' found under the plant tubers can be eaten raw after scraping or peeled and boiled in broth
Habitat: Hedgerows, open woodlands, banks, roadsides, rough grassy places, heaths

Scentless Mayweed *Tripleurospermum inodorum (Matricaria inodorum)*

Perennial with hairless leaves and smooth spreading stems up to 60cm long. White large daisy flower-heads, the bracts around which are brown edged. Named not from the month of May but from the Old English word for maiden. Matricaria is from the Latin for womb

Flowers: July-September
Habitat: Common in grassy places

Sea Campion *Silene uniflora*

Perennial, woody at the base with outward spreading stems, growing along the ground. Leaves smaller and stiffer than *Bladder Campion*, with fewer long-stalked flowers on each stem. Not to be confused with white forms of the *Red Campion*

Flowers: May-September
Local Names: White Snap-jacks
Habitat: Common around the coastal cliffs and shingly beach areas. Patches of the plant will be found along the South West Coast Path

Snowdrop *Galanthus nivalis*

Long slender green leaves forming at the base of the plant and white nodding flower heads. There are green markings on the petals. The plant is hairless and grows from bulbs. Snowdrops grow in clumps 10-20cm

Flowers: Jan-March
Local Names: Snowbells
Habitat: Woodland, coppices, hedgerows, grassy places

Three Cornered Leek *Allium triquetrum*

An introduced species, now naturalised. Not unlike a white bluebell, the three cornered leek has white bell-like flowers which droop from the one-sided umbel arrangement. However it is easily identified by its triangular (three cornered) stalks. The plant smells of garlic if crushed. The leaves are long slim and glossy. Grows from bulbs and can be invasive. Inhabits heavy soils
Flowers: April-June
Habitat: Grassy places, open woodlands, hedgerows, waste places

White Clover *Trifolium repens*

Small, hairless perennial with creeping and rooting stems. Grows 8-20cm high. Finely toothed leaflets show a pale band across. Very common. Used in cultivation in grassland pastures. Three in one leaves and four leaved clovers are lucky
Flowers: June-September
Local Names: Bee bread, Broad-grass, Claver, Baa-lambs, Bobby Roses, Mull, and Three Leaved Grass
Habitat: Grassy places

Wild Carrot *Daucus carota*

Growing 50-100cm, it has divided leaves which are fern-like. The stems are erect and often branched. Flowers form on long stems and have lacy heads
Flowers: June-August
Ancient Uses: Used against fainting. Wild carrot was also eaten as a vegetable
Habitat: Hedgebanks, railway embankments, rough grassland, roadside verges, waste ground, downs, cliffs, dry meadows

Wild Clematis *Clematis vitalba*

A rampant deciduous plant which climbs by twisting its leaf stalks around the stems of other plants. The flowers are a whitish green or cream colour and are fragrantly sweet
Flowers: July-September
Local Names: Grandfather's Whiskers, Old Man's Beard, Gipsy's Bacca
Ancient Uses: Rubbed on travellers' bruises to ease aches and pains
Habitat: Scrub, woodland, hedgerows

Wild Garlic or Ramsons *Allium ursinum*

A strong smelling plant. Flower heads are clustered with white star-shaped flowers. Plant grows 25-45cm high
Flowers: April-June
Local Names: Ramsons, Ramsey
Ancient Uses: Country fish sauce was made from the leaves. Bulbs pickled in rum were used against chesty coughs
Habitat: Hedgerows, deciduous woodlands, scrub, coppices, meadows and banks which are partly shaded

Wild Strawberry *Fragaria vesca*

Bright green leaves are toothed, stalked and have three leaflets. Hairy plant with slender, erect and branched flower stems. There are five white petals to each yellow centred flower. Grows 10-25cm. Bears the tiny fruits in late summer
Flowers: April-July
Ancient Uses: The fruit is used to make jam or is eaten fresh with sugar and cream
Habitat: Hedgerows, woodlands, roadsides, embankments, scrub

Wood Anemone *Anemone nemorosa*

Grows 5-30cm, in patches. The leaves which form in whorls of three, have three deep lobes. The flowers nod in the slightest breeze and are usually white but may sometimes be purple/lilac to bluish. They close up in the late afternoon and open when the sun rises the following day

Flowers: March-May

Local Names: Windflower

Habitat: Hedgerows, scrub, woodland, coppices

Wood Sorrel *Oxalis acetosella*

A perennial growing 4-10cm high. Drooping leaves with each of the three leaflets being heart-shaped. Loosely bell-shaped white flowers sometimes showing lilac or mauve veins. Wood Sorrel grows in clumps or patches

Flowers: April-June

Local Names: Rabbit's Meat, Bread-and-Cheese

Ancient Uses: The leaves were eaten raw or put into a green sauce

Habitat: Woodlands, hedgerows and humus-rich habitats

Yarrow *Achillea millefolium*

Hairy grey-green foliage. Flowers are usually white but sometimes pink-red. The small, numerous flowers on separate branched flower heads make up large flat blossoms. Yarrow grows in patches

Flowers: July-October

Local Names: Woundwort

Ancient Uses: Used on wounds particularly those caused by iron

Habitat: Grassy banks, meadows, roadsides, hedgerows

Alexanders *Smyrnium olusatrum*

Rare inland but not uncommon around the coastal areas. A tall biennial 60-120cm high with solid, furrowed stems which have a celery taste when young. Flowers are more yellow than most umbellifers and the fruits are almost black and sharply ribbed
Flowers: April-June
Local Names: Hell Root, Wild Celery
Ancient Uses: An ancient pot herb, originally naturalised from the Mediterranean
Habitat: Cliffs and waste places near the sea

Dog's Mercury *Mercurialis perennis*

Small green-yellow flowers on a long stalk. Leaves are finely toothed - makes good ground cover growing 15-40cm high and spreading via its creeping roots
Flowers: February- April
Local Names: Boggart Flower
Ancient Uses: Poisonous but various parts of the plant were used to make dyes. Used on swollen weeping sores and warts
Habitat: Deciduous woodlands and old hedgerows in particular

Wild Arum *Arum maculatum*

Grows 15-35cm. Hairless and fleshy with long stalked, untoothed arrow-shaped leaves which are often covered in dark blotches. The flower is a chocolate brown spike enclosed in a large pointed hood or spathe
Flowers: April-May
Local Names: Lords and Ladies, Cuckoo Pint, Adder's Meat, Adder's Tongue, Jack-in-the-pulpit, Toad's Meat, Wake Robin
Habitat: Woods, hedgerows, scrub, wooded cliffs, occasionally on cultivated land

Portland Spurge *Euphorbia portlandica*

Less tall and robust than the similar *Sea Spurge* (see below), and greyer in colour. Leaves are small, egg-shaped with pointed tips, tapering towards the base and are leathery. Usually has a reddish tinge to the stem and lower leaves

Flowers: May-September

Habitat: Coastal grasslands and rocks, sea cliffs and sand dunes

Sea Spurge *Euphorbia paralias*

The waxy green leaves of this perennial are thick, fleshy untoothed, stalkless and crowded together on the stems. Flowers have clusters of 3-6 main branches and the rounded bracts are also thick and fleshy

Flowers: July-October

Habitat: Young sand dunes, sandy shores and occasionally on fine shingle

Wall Pennywort *Umbilicus rupestris*

Wall pennywort grows between 15-40cm. Flowers are small, bell-shaped and numerous to make up flower spikes. Flowers are cream or pale greenish-white. Leaves are round and fleshy

Flowers: June-August

Local Names: Navel Wort, Cups-and-Saucers, Penny Loaves, Milk-the-Cows

Ancient Uses: For cuts and chilblains

Habitat: Walls, dry sandy hedge banks, and on mossy oak tree bases

Yellow Flag Iris

Bird's Foot Trefoil *Lotus corniculatus*

A brightly golden flower often tinged flame-like, with leaves with five oval leaflets. The lowest leaflet pair is close to the stem, distant from the other three. Flowers in 'heads' of 3-8.
Flowers: June-August
Local Names: Bird's Claws, Bunny Rabbits, Butter and Eggs, Cammock, Cuckoo's Stockings, Lady's Cushion. There are over a hundred local names in Britain for this plant
Habitat: Dry grassland areas, the plant carpeting the coastal walks in parts of Cornwall

Broom *Cytisus scoparius*

An erect, hairless shrub not unlike gorse, but lacking the spines. The bright yellow pea flowers cluster the stalks
Flowers: April-June
Local Names: Banathel, Banathal, Bannel
Ancient Uses: Used in wine-making and also, as its name suggests, to make brooms. If sheep are allowed to nibble broom they say it keeps 'the rot' away
Habitat: Open Woodlands, grassy places, hedge banks, scrub and heaths

Bulbous Buttercup *Ranunculus bulbosus*

Growing up to 40cm, it is a perennial, erect and hairy plant with a grooved stem. Bright yellow flowers with visibly down-turned sepals. Named after its bulbous base. Leaves at the base of the plant are long stalked, toothed with three lobes
Flowers: May-July
Ancient Uses: Used to produce blisters and to draw out nasties, possibly used during the time of the plague along with other members of the buttercup family
Habitat: Dry pastures and grassy areas

Coltsfoot *Tussilago farfara*

The bright golden flowers are daisy-like. The stems are fleshy, stocky and covered in purplish scales. Grows 10-25cm. Leaves appear after flowering

Flowers: February-April

Local Names: Poor Man's Baccy

Ancient Uses: An infusion of leaves can be taken for dry coughs and bronchitis

Habitat: Roadside verges, hedge banks, waste ground, cultivated land, embankments, scree, damp sites

Common Agrimony *Agrimonia eupatoria*

A gracefully slender plant growing 50-100cm. Hairy, with erect stems and a slender spike of yellow flowers. Each tiny flower has five petals. Leaves are alternate and toothed, and there are 3-6 main pairs of leaflets to each

Flowers: June-August

Local Names: Salt-and-Pepper

Ancient Uses: Against snake bites, dysentery and liver problems. Agrimony wine is used for colds; agrimony tea is good as a tonic

Habitat: Hedgerows, wood edges, grassy verges and railway embankments

Cow-wheat *Melampyrum pratense*

Common Cow-wheat has the distinguishing characteristic that all its flowers face the same way. The flowers are deep yellow to almost white. Grows 15-30cm

Flowers: May-September

Ancient Uses: Cow-wheat flour was believed to be an aphrodisiac; some believed it caused women to give birth to boys.

Habitat: Common in woods, on moors, and found around the coast near trees

Cowslip *Primula veris*

Cowslips have clusters of drooping flowers with bell-shaped calyx and notched petal lobes of deep golden-yellow. Grows 10-30cm. Long, slender, erect stems with a rosette of primrose shaped leaves at its base

Flowers: April-May

Local Names: Cuckoo

Ancient Uses: Against palsy or paralysis and used to make country wines

Habitat: Dry open grassy places alongside roads, in meadows and on banks

Daffodil *Narcissus pseudonarcissus*

Large nodding yellow flowers with six petal segments and a deeper yellow-orange central trumpet-shaped corolla. Solitary flowers and long narrow linear leaves forming at the base of the plant. Chiefly the flower we tend to use for Mother's Day and in churches for Lent

Flowers: April-May

Local Names: Lent Lily, Daffydowndilly.

Habitat: Woods, banks and meadows

Dandelion *Taraxacum officinale*

Growing 5-30cm high with a rosette of long deeply toothed leaves. Flowers are large and bright golden-yellow with slender erect stems

Flowers: March-October

Local Names: Believed to have come from the French *dent de lion* - lion's tooth

Ancient Uses: The young leaves were eaten raw in salads being good for the complexion and full of vitamin A and C

Habitat: Lawns, waste ground, meadows and roadside verges

Evening Primrose *Oenothera biennis*

Erect, usually unbranched, grows 80-150cm.
Leaves oval, lance-shaped, often toothed.
Flowers saucer-shaped, bright yellow and
large, usually falling after a day's blooming
to be replaced by others
Flowers: June-September
Ancient Uses: Against whooping cough,
asthma, female complaints, gastro-intestinal
disorders
Habitats: Sandy places around the coast,
roadsides, open habitats, waste ground and
disturbed ground

Common Fleabane *Pulicaria dysenterica*

Densely hairy, the alternate leaves are greyish
underneath, arrow-shaped and unstalked.
The bottom lower leaves are oval with a
narrow base, whilst stem leaves have
clasping stems. The flowers are bright yellow,
daisy-like, forming in branched clusters.
Petals are numerous and short
Local Names: Harvest flower
Ancient Uses: To deter midges and fleas
Habitat: Hedgerows, ditches, alongside
streams and wet meadows

Gorse *Ulex europaeus*

Gorse grows up to 2.5m high and flowers
may be found at all times of the year
although April-June is when gorse flowers at
its peak. Flowers are a deep rich yellow
Local Names: Honey Bottle, Pins & Needles,
Thumbs & Fingers
Ancient Uses: Fuel for bakers, brick makers,
lime burners and farmer's wives. Crushed
spines of gorse provided winter feed for
livestock
Habitat: Rough grassy places and heaths

Great Mullein *Verbascum thapsus*

Growing from 1-2m, it has yellow flowers clustered to form a narrow spike, and large downy leaves, the whole plant being covered with whitish or greyish soft hairs
Flowers: June-August
Local Names: Fluff-Weed, Flannel Plant
Ancient Uses: The stalks dipped in suet were used to burn at country funerals
Habitat: Found on dry soils in sunny places, especially in rough dry grassland, waste sites, hedge banks and roadsides

Hop Trefoil *Trifolium campestre*

Like *Clover*, it is trifoliate with finely toothed leaves and has stipules at the leaf bases. Flowers have stalks and are small dense yellow clusters in rounded heads. A hairy plant usually with spreading stems
Flowers: June-September
Habitat: Dry grassy places, sand dunes, bare ground and scrub

Kidney Vetch *Anthyllis vulneraria*

Low growing plant. When growing near the sea the flowers may vary from pale yellow to orange and fiery red
Flowers: May-August
Local Names: Lady's Fingers, Hens and Chickens.
Ancient Uses: Known throughout Europe as a wound herb or 'vulnerary'.
Habitat: Often common in dry grassy habitats near the sea and may carpet whole areas in golden patches

Lesser Celandine *Ranunculus ficaria*

Plant has short fleshy stems and heart-shaped leaves. It grows 5-25cm high. Flowers are bright yellow, star-like and commonly known as 'the first herald of spring'
Flowers: March-May
Local Names: Pilewort
Ancient Uses: Used to treat problems of cow's udders. Used against piles and corns, and effective as a skin cleanser
Habitat: Hedgerows, damp grassy places, ditches, streams and woodlands

Marsh Marigold *Caltha palustris*

Kidney-heart shaped leaves that are deeply toothed and deeply lobed with 5-7 segments. A hairless plant with branched flower clusters. Flowers are large like open over-sized buttercups, saucer-shaped and are deeply golden yellow
Flowers: March-August
Local Names: King Cups, May Blobs
Habitat: Wet areas such as marshes, stream margins, bogs, wet woodland

Meadow Buttercup *Ranunculus acris*

Lower leaves are deeply divided, stalked and toothed. Stems are branched bearing lovely golden buttercups with five petals. Grows 30-90cm
Flowers: May-September
Ancient Uses: Against lunacy (sympathetic magic)
Habitat: Damp meadows and grassy places

Meadow Vetchling *Lathyrus pratensis*

Yellow pea flowers with five to twelve in each long stalked head. Leaflets are narrow and spear-shaped with one pair per leaf. Leaves are alternate and have tendrils the plant uses to clamber over other vegetation. Grows 50-120cm
Flowers: May-August
Habitat: Rough grassland, roadsides, hedgerows, coastal areas, scrub

Pineapple Weed *Chamomilla suaveolens* (*Matricaria discoidea*)

Alien now naturalised. The yellow-green heads smell distinctively of pineapples when pinched. Petal-less, divided, feathery leaves, divided stems, upright and hairless
Flowers: May-November
Local Names: Ray-less Mayweed
Habitat: Waste places, pavements, sides of roads and paths

Primrose *Primula vulgaris*

The primrose has very pale yellow flowers, rarely pink or white. Growing 5-12cm high, it is soft haired and has flowers on slender stalks. The leaves are bright green, oblong and form rosettes at the base of the plant
Flowers: January-May
Ancient Uses: Used to cure yellow jaundice, skin complaints, ring-worm, burns and scalds
Habitat: Grassy places, hedge banks, open woodland, meadows, ditches and roadsides

Ragwort *Senecio jacobaea*

Perennial growing 120cm, with a rosette of large divided leaves at the base which often dies before the plant flowers. Officially a noxious weed, dangerous to horses and livestock, but not usually eaten by animals. Bright yellow daisy-like flowers

Flowers: June-October

Habitat: Hedgerows, roadsides, river embankments, meadows, pastures, waste land, sand dunes, coastal shingle

Silverweed *Potentilla anserina*

Leaves grow in a rosette at the base of the plant, are grey-green but silver underneath hence silverweed. Each leaf is made up of 15-25 oblong, toothed leaflets. Flowers are rich yellow with usually five petals

Flowers: May-August

Ancient Uses: The root of silverweed was said to have been cultivated before the introduction of the potato

Habitat: Cultivated land, waste places, pathways and sand dunes

St John's Wort *Hypericum perforatum*

Grows 40-80cm. Flowers are yellow and have five petals with many stamens in the centres. They have no nectar

Flowers: May-September

Ancient Uses: To cure catarrh, grow hair, heal cuts and cure sprains. Also used against poisons, to heal burns and in early cultures, to ward off evil. The plant is named after St John the Baptist

Habitat: Hedgerows, banks, roadside verges, woods, scrub and other grassy places

Tansy *Tanacetum vulgare*

Erect stems with deep yellow-orange button-like flowers in dense clusters. Finely divided fern-like leaves

Flowers: July-September
Local Names: Bachelor's Buttons
Ancient Uses: Against miscarriages; and worms in children. As a substitute for spices in cooking. To repel mice from corn and bluebottles from meat
Habitat: Scrub, grassy places, hedgerows, roadsides and river banks

Western Gorse *Ulex gallii*

This is very much a West Country gorse and smaller than the common species, growing up to 60cm. It is extremely shiny with deep golden yellow to orange flowers. The best flowering period is from July-September but it continues to flower in less profusion throughout the year, hence the saying, 'When Gorse is out of flower, kissing's out of season'
Habitat: Acid soil, rough grassland, often found growing with heather

Yellow Stonecrop *Sedum acre*

The plant forms mats of short stems 5-10cm. Strikingly yellow and the commonest and smallest of the stonecrops. A fleshy plant with alternate, egg-shaped leaves which taste peppery

Flowers: May-July
Ancient Uses: Against scurvy, dropsy and some fevers
Habitats: Sandy places around the coast. On rocks and walls near the sea as well as shingle beaches

Monkshood

Bittersweet *Solanum dulcamara*

The nodding flowers are usually purple with a bright yellow cone-shaped stamen. A scrambling, climbing plant without tendrils, growing 1-4m high. May be found sprawling over the ground. Fruits are clusters of green berries which turn yellow-orange-red as they ripen
Flowers: June-September
Local Names: Fool's Cap, Felonwood
Ancient Uses: Against dizziness and vertigo
Habitat: On beaches, sand dunes, woods and hedgerows

Bluebell *Hyacinthoides non-scripta*

Often grows in clumps and the stems curve at the top part of the plant where the blue-violet, bell-shaped flowers begin to form. Spanish bluebells are rather sturdier and more erect. Shiny, long, narrow leaves
Flowers: May-June
Local Names: Wild Hyacinth, Cuckoo Flower
Ancient Uses: Both glue and starch were made from the bulbs. Today it is illegal to uproot the bulbs of the bluebell
Habitat: Woodlands, copses and hedge banks. Under threat by the Spanish Bluebell

Brooklime *Veronica beccabunga*

Fleshy hairless plant with opposite, toothed, short-stalked leaves. Flowers are usually pale to deep blue with white centres
Flowers: May-September
Local Names: Bird's Eye
Ancient Uses: Against tumours, inflammation and swellings and as a cure for scurvy. The young shoots were used in salads and diet drinks were also made from the plant
Habitat: Wet mud near streams, rivers ditches and wet meadows

Bugle *Ajuga reptans*

A perennial growing 10-30cm high with whorls of blue, occasionally pink or white flowers. Leaves and stems may take on a bluish-purple or bronze tinge mixed with dark green
Flowers: April-June
Local Names: Thunder-and-Lightning
Ancient Uses: Used against ulcers and broken bones
Habitat: Shady places, damp woodlands and grasslands

Chicory *Cichorium intybus*

The flowers are usually bright blue. The upper leaves have no stalks and clasp the stem whereas the lower leaves have stalks, being similar to those of the dandelion in shape. A perennial growing 60-120cm
Flowers: July-October
Ancient Uses: Used as a purgative. Water around the flowers helped dimmed eye-sight The dried root is added to some coffee blends
Habitat: Waste places, fields and rough grassland, roadside verges

Dog Violet *Viola riviniana*

The flowers of the Common Dog Violet have no scent but are a deep violet blue. The leaves have long stalks and are heart-shaped and gently toothed. The plant grows 8-20cm, and avoids wet conditions
Flowers: April-June, although it may flower again at the end of summer
Ancient Uses: Used against cancer. The juice from boiled violets was used for headaches
Habitat: Hedgebanks, open deciduous woodland, grassy places and heaths

Germander Speedwell *Veronica chamaedrys*

Bright blue flowers are quite small measuring 9-12mm across. The oval leaves are almost triangular. Plant grows 20-40cm
Flowers: March-July
Local Names: Cat's Eyes
Ancient Uses: Cure for jaundice and as a tea, for indigestion and pains in the stomach
Habitat: Hedgerows, embankments, grassy areas, road and lane verges, woodland borders, damp stony ground

Green Alkanet *Pentaglottis sempervirens*

Grows 50-100cm. A bristly, leafy, erect plant with branched stems. Leaves are untoothed, have a narrow base and are oval to spear-shaped. Flowers are bright blue, spiralled and clustered
Flowers: April-July
Ancient Uses: Roots produce a red dye
Habitat: Shaded hedge banks, damp woodland, borders, grassy and waste places. Often found growing near buildings

Monk's-hood *Aconitum napellus*

Growing 80-150cm high, Monkshood has stiff erect stems and usually deep blue-violet flowers shaped like hoods. Alternate leaves divided into lobes of 5-7 giving a thick feathery or shredded appearance. Pollinated by bees
Flowers: June-September
Local Names: Old Woman's Nightcap
Ancient Uses: Used as a poison
Habitat: Shaded stream banks, damp woodlands, scrub and meadows

Self-heal *Prunella vulgaris*

Grows 15-30cm high and is covered with tiny hairs. Flowers are purple or bluish violet, and are clustered in dense, oblong-shaped heads
Flowers: June-November
Ancient Uses: A woodland herb, used to stem blood flow. Chosen by modern herbalists as a useful astringent
Habitat: Hedgerows, grassy places, roadsides, open woodlands, woodland tracks and clearings

Tufted Vetch *Vicia cracca*

Slender, branch stems with 6-15 pairs of narrow leaflets. At the end of each leaf, tendrils twine themselves around vegetation, enabling the plant to climb and clamber some distance. The purplish blue flowers form in long dense heads. Related to the pea family. Plant grows 80-200cm high
Flowers: June-August
Ancient Uses: Against small pox and measles
Habitat: Hedgerows, grassy places, scrub, roadsides, woodland margins, coastal areas

Viper's Bugloss *Echium vulgare*

Tall vivid blue biennial 30-90cm high, covered with white bristly hairs. Rosettes of large, stalked leaves may wither before flowering. Flowers have pink buds. Visited by insects for nectar
Flowers: June-September
Local Names: Blue Devil, Blue Thistle, Cat's Tail, Wild Borage. It is called 'Viper's' because the nutlets resemble a viper's head
Ancient Uses: Against snake bites, sadness and melancholy
Habitat: Common in coastal dunes

Red Poppies

Dodder *Cuscuta epithymum*

Thin leafless stems giving an overall reddish appearance, twining anti-clockwise, usually over gorse and heather. Tiny pinkish flowers. A parasite attached by suckers to the stems of host species. Locally common
Flowers: July-October
Local Name: Epiphany
Ancient Uses: Against scabies, and as a purgative
Habitat: Coastal cliffs and heaths wherever its host plants grow. Found growing over the host plants in a tangle

Hedge Woundwort *Stachys sylvatica*

Grows 60-100cm. Has square, erect stems and is softly hairy. The paired leaves with short stalks are coarsely toothed, narrow to broadly heart-shaped and pointed, rather like the leaves of the nettle. The basal leaves are long stalked. Spikes of flowers are reddish-purple, with whorls forming at the base of the upper leaves
Flowers: June-September
Habitat: Hedgerows, roadsides, waste ground, woodland

Houndstongue *Cynoglossum officinale*

Houndstongue grows up to 40-70cm high. It is covered in long silky hairs and is soft to touch. Flowers are blood purple-red
Flowers: June to August
Local Names: Sticky Buds
Ancient Uses: Used against dog bites, burns, baldness, internal sores and ulcers, skin diseases and piles
Habitats: Waste ground or by roadsides and hedges, edges of woods, sand dunes and downs by the sea

Red Campion *Silene dioica*

The leaves are untoothed, oblong to oval, and the lower leaves have stalks. A hairy plant, erect, with unscented deep pink flowers, it grows 50-100cm
Flowers: May-November
Local Names: Dolly Winter, Fleabites, Red Riding Hood, Bob Robin, Cock Robin, Red Robin, Robin Hood, Robin Red-breast
Habitat: Deciduous woodland, woodland clearings, hedge banks, hedgerows, cliff ledges and scree

Red Clover *Trifolium pratense*

Reddish-purple or pink flowers forming in dense rounded heads directly above pairs of leaves. Grows 20-60cm and often cultivated as animal fodder. Attracts honey bees
Flowers: May-September
Local Names: Bee-bread, Cow-cloos, Claver
Ancient Uses: Used to fertilise the soil with nitrogen, to cure whooping cough, to make country wine and to ward off evil
Habitat: Grassy places, cultivated ground, roadside verges, waste ground

Red Poppies *Papaver rhoeas*

Growing up to 60cm. Bright scarlet flowers. The 'Poppy Day' poppy once common in corn fields, but mostly destroyed by weed killers
Flowers: June-August
Local Names: Bull's Eye, Butterfly Ladies, Cornflower, Corn Rose, Cheesebowls, Headache, Red Nap, Thunderbolt
Ancient Uses: Used to cure headaches. Placed in roof timbers to ward off lightning
Habitat: Waste places, roadsides, cultivated land and field edges

Redshank *Persicaria maculosa* (also called *Polygonum persicaria*)

Grows 20-80cm, a perennial with numerous small deep pink or pale pink flowers forming in short, dense, compact heads. Leaves are downy underneath, alternate, spear-shaped and usually bear a dark patch. An erect plant with branching stems
Flowers: June-October
Habitat: Waste ground, cultivated land, railways, roadsides and often by ponds and streams

Red Valerian *Centranthus ruber*

A stout, rather fleshy plant with thick, erect stems 50-80cm in height. The leaves are grey-green or bluish-green. Flowers can be red, pink or white and form in dense fluffy heads
Flowers: June-August
Local Names: Fowey Pride, Ladies' Needlework, Pride of Padstow, Saucy Bet
Ancient Uses: Young leaves can be mixed into a salad or boiled and shaken up with butter
Habitat: Stony open hedges, walls, rocks, cliffs, dry sunny or sandy sites, stony waste ground

Scarlet Pimpernel *Anagallis arvensis*

Flowers have 5 petals, are red, occasionally pink-lilac, white or blue. Flowers close in dull weather, and also each evening to re-open next morning
Flowers: May-October
Local Names: Grandfather's Weatherglass, Weatherglass
Ancient Uses: Against toothache, snakebite, melancholy, liver and kidney troubles and hydrophobia
Habitat: Waste ground, path-sides, dunes, cultivated land, light sandy or chalky soils

INDEX

INDEX

GLOSSARY

Axil.................Where a leaf or stalk joins the stem

Bract...............A small leaf immediately beneath a flower or cluster of flowers

Calyx..............Outer ring of components of a flower, often divided into separate sepals

Corolla..........Conspicuous component of most flowers, lying inside the sepals and usually brightly coloured. Often divided into separate petals

Lanceolate.....Narrow pointed leaf shape like a lance or spear

Sepals.............The part of the plant that encloses the flower bud

Stipule............Small, often leaf-like appendage at the base of the leaf stalk

Trifoliate........A 'three leaved' leaf shape

Umbel...........Umbrella shaped compound flower head in which all the flowers are borne on stalks arising like umbrella spokes from a single point